The Essential Guide To Success Checklist

The Essential Guide To Success Checklist

The 30-Day Challenge to Build Your Path to Success
and Fulfil Your Life's Purpose

Pascale D. Gibon

Providence Publishing Ltd
London, England

www.pascalegibon.com

Copyright © 2017 by Pascale D. Gibon

For permission request contact:
Providence Publishing Ltd
25 Glazbury road
London, W14 9AS
support@pascalegibon.com

The Essential Guide To Success Checklist
The 30-Day Challenge to Build Your Path to Success and Fulfil Your Life's Purpose

ISBN 978-0-9935198-2-6 (print edition)

This book may be purchased for educational, business or sales promotional use. For information about special discounts for bulk purchases please contact support@pascalegibon.com

Printed in the United Kingdom

Visit us online at: www.pascalegibon.com

*I dedicate The Essential Guide To Success
Checklist to my mum who taught me to always
follow my dreams and to those who believe in love and
service and want to share their voice with the world purposefully.*

CONTENTS

Introduction 1

Day 1 What is success? 4

Day 2 Love what you do and do what you love 6

Day 3 Successful people do things in a certain way 9

Day 4 Take 100% responsibility for your results 11

Day 5 You become what you think about 13

Day 6 Your thoughts, feelings and actions create your results 16

Day 7 What do you want? 18

Day 8 3 ways to catapult your results 21

Day 9 How to overcome obstacles on the way 24

Day 10 Feel the fear and do it anyway 27

Day 11 Be willing to be uncomfortable 29

Day 12 Declutter your mind 31

Day 13 Create the right supportive environment 34

Day 14 Clear up your messes 38

Day 15 Clear up your incompletes 40

Day 16 Cultivate a success mindset 42

Day 17 Create an action mindset 44

Day 18 Map out your clear goals 46

Day 19 Map out your action steps 48

Day 20 Identify your resources 50

Day 21 Ask for what you want 52

Day 22 Mastermind your way to success 54

Day 23 Achieve your goals 56

Day 24 Stay focused 58

Day 25 Manage your activities effectively 60

Day 26 Monitor your progress 62

Day 27 Be disciplined 64

Day 28 Rinse and repeat the cycle of excellence 67

Day 29 Be grateful 69

Day 30 Celebrate your successes 71

Summary Of The Success Checklist Activities 73

Special invitation from Pascale 78

About Pascale Gibon 80

Other Resources 81

Acknowledgments 82

YOUR FREE GIFT

As a thank you for your purchase and support, I have a special gift for you which would be a great companion to this journal. My 3-part video course on how to achieve your dreams entitled: 'The 7 Key Principles to Achieve Your Dreams.'

You can get access to the FREE 3-part video course today.

Access your FREE gift here: http://bit.ly/DCLvideos.

To your success and happiness!

With love and gratitude

Pascale Gibon

Your Change Catalyst

INTRODUCTION

If you are reading The Essential Guide To Success Checklist - The 30-Day Challenge to Build Your Path to Success and Fulfil Your Life's Purpose, it means that you have raised your hand to say that you are committed and ready to stand out and shine, to give with love from a place of service, to expand your world and your mind, to explore new possibilities, to play a bigger game, to be significant, to fulfil your dreams, to become the best that you can be and to live a life of purpose and meaning.

Since you aspire to live the life that you truly desire by fulfilling your dreams, you are also ready to transform and to improve your results. However, in order to be the best that you can be authentically you have to be willing to be honest with yourself, to do things differently, and to adopt the right attitude for success. I believe that you are willing; you would not have picked up the Essential Guide To Success Checklist otherwise.

In this journal, I reveal the secrets to reaching a higher level of achievement so that you can take your life's purpose to the next level.

Perhaps you have a great vision, big dreams and goals, but you are not on the path to success yet because there are missing pieces to your success puzzle.

In this Essential Guide To Success Checklist I set you on a 30-day challenge so that you can embark on the path to success, get better results and live the life you desire.

I come from a lineage of solo-preneurs and entrepreneurs; therefore, I stand on the shoulders of giants who have shown me that I can choose to create and live the life that I desire.

As a Licensed LifeSuccess Consultant, a Master Results Coach, a Certified Jack Canfield Trainer in the Success Principles, a Transformational Success Life Coach and Trainer and a Passion Test Facilitator, I have been fascinated by the subject of success and in particular what makes someone successful or not.

My conclusion is that it takes courage, confidence and leadership to achieve success. Do not believe anyone who tells you that it is easy. In fact, it requires effort and keeping abreast of excellence. A good example are athletes who compete for the Olympics: it takes hours and hours of training for an athlete to win a gold medal. Success is never achieved alone, without effort or a tested and proven system. It requires also strong positive beliefs, faith, attitude, motivation and passion.

Is it worth it? YES! absolutely because of the personal fulfilment it brings. You experience growth whenever you set yourself a goal: are you willing to embark on a journey of self-discovery and development? If your answer is YES! continue reading...

How to use this journal

The Essential Guide To Success Checklist is both a guide and a journal. It has been designed for you to develop a new success idea daily as you learn a new principle for success. Every day you will learn, work on and apply a success principle. Through this step by step process, each daily lesson will become clear and imbedded into your consciousness and awareness.

As you go through this material daily you create a new paradigm. Your paradigm is your attitude, behaviour or multitude of habits. In order for you to achieve success and change your results, you must create a new paradigm to get to where you want to be since you cannot use the same paradigm, which has been keeping you stuck.

As you embark on The 30-Day Challenge to Build Your Path to Success and Fulfil Your Life's Purpose, you will set shifts in motion and achieve the following:

- Gain greater clarity with regard to where you are and where you want to be

- Create a new paradigm for success

- Draw a clear plan for success

- Develop the right success mindset

- Develop the right action mindset

- Get the results that you desire

- Become unstoppable

I also recommend that you get a personal journal for greater and deeper reflection. Writing your thoughts down will encourage creativity and help you progress and see clearly the changes you need to make.

I believe in you and I wish you success. I am convinced that when you play full on, you learn and apply the daily success principles contained in the Essential Guide To Success Checklist, then you can change your results into impactful and positive ones and change your life.

To your success and happiness!

With love and gratitude

Pascale Gibon

What is success?

"Success is the progressive realization of a worthy ideal."

–Earl Nightingale

Human beings are motivated by three things:

- Power: the desire to be in control of their life

- Affiliation: the desire to love and be loved

- Achievement: the desire to achieve their goals.

You cannot dissociate power, affiliation and achievement as you embark on the road to success because they are all important and they motivate you to reach your destination.

Ultimately, however, since you have decided to follow the path to success and to fulfil your life's purpose you have chosen to self-realize or to attain ultimate freedom. I describe ultimate freedom as the desire to be the full expression of love, joy and happiness from the inside out, for no reason. Additionally, ultimate freedom is the desire for fulfilment, well-being, gratification, purpose and meaning.

In this light, my best definition of success is from Earl Nightingale: "Success is the progressive realization of a worthy ideal." In his quote, the word ideal stands for goal. Therefore, success is the progressive realisation of a worthy goal. Success is a journey, and the journey to success can be a long road, depending on what you wish to achieve. When we consider Earl Nightingale's definition of success, your goal is worth pursuing and accomplishing because it will require a lot of your own energy, time and passion. Thus, you must have a goal which is worthy of you.

Action step: what does success mean to you?

....

....

....

....

....

....

....

....

....

....

Love what you do and do what you love

"Let the beauty we love be what we do."

–Rumi

It is highly recognised that it is easier to achieve success when you do something that you love. Indeed, when you do something that you love you are what we call 'in flow' or in total alignment with what your heart and soul desire. As a consequence, you are authentic and answering your true calling. You are not called to do something for convenience sake because it is comfortable and it is safe but to do something that enlightens you, makes you feel alive and brings you the greatest joy. You cannot wait to get up in the morning and get started on your mission for the day because you love what you do and you love who you are being.

Doing things with passion means that you strive for your highest ideal.

☐

Action step: what are you passionate about?

....

....

....

....

....

....

....

....

....

....

....

....

....

....

....

☐

Action step: do you currently do what you love?

☐ Yes

☐ No

If your answer is no, what would ignite your passion and purpose?

....

....

....

....

....

....

....

....

....

....

....

....

DAY 3

Successful people do things in a certain way

"The Secret to Success: find something you love to do so much, you can't wait for the sun to rise to do it all over again."

–Chris Gardner

Every successful person will tell you that you do not need to re-invent the wheel and that a very effective way of achieving success is to model the people who stand before you and succeed.

There is no greater example than someone who has done the same thing that you want to do and succeeded at it. Of course, as you stand on the shoulders of giants, you bring in your own creativity and uniqueness, while also following their principles, strategies, and techniques for success.

In order to ensure your progress, you can model someone who has succeeded in what you want to achieve, and this could be in any area of your life: finances, personal life, spirituality, career, health and fun.

Pascale D. Gibon

☐

Action step: who are the successful people you could model?

....

....

....

....

....

....

....

....

....

....

....

....

....

....

....

....

DAY 4

Take 100% responsibility for your results

"Follow the three R's: Respect for self, - Respect for others, - Responsibility for all of your actions."

–Dalai Lama

When you take 100% responsibility for your results, you become the leader of your life. You would be in control over your life.

The law of cause and effect dictates that you are at cause when you take 100% responsibility for your life and results, and you are at effect when you blame others. Therefore, when you blame your circumstances, your environment on others, then you effectively say that you cannot change your circumstances, your environment and your results because it is not your responsibility. It is worth pointing out, however, that when you blame others, your environment and your circumstances it is because you can actually change it.

Taking 100% responsibility for your results is very empowering. It means that you choose to respond to your situation by re-evaluating where you are: thinking about what you could do differently and planning the achievement of better results. When you choose to do whatever is necessary to change your life and your results you are not comfortable with the status quo, and you take 100% responsibility.

☐

> *Commit to taking 100% responsibility for your life and results*

Exercise: Your 100% Responsibility Commitment Statement

"I am so happy and grateful now that I take 100% responsibility for my life and results"

Signature: ....

Date: ....

You become what you think about

"Your results are a physical or outward expression of the inner conditioning in your subconscious mind."

–Bob Proctor

Your mind is powerful and can dictate the course of your life. Over the course of history, scientists, philosophers, theologians, the great wise men, teachers and prophets agreed upon one thing: 'We literally become what we think about.'

In order to achieve success, it is essential that your thoughts, feelings and actions are in alignment and supportive of the image for change you have in mind.

Understanding your thought process as a human being will transform your life and help you become aware of why certain things happen in a particular way.

Your thought process as a human being is as follows:

- Your results are caused by your thoughts

- Your thoughts cause your feelings

- Your feelings cause your actions

- Your actions give you particular results

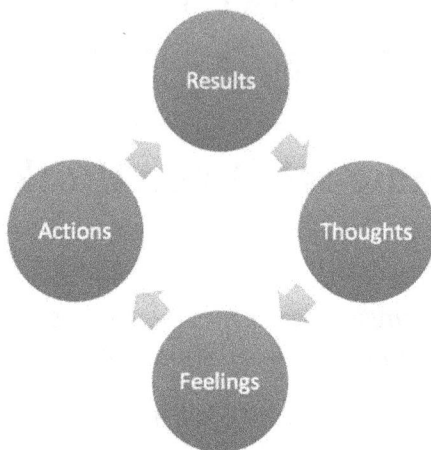

Exercise: Your Thought Process

I want you to think for a moment of a particular result you get in an area of your life, that you are not happy with.

- What are your thoughts, feelings and actions when you consider this particular area of your life?

As such, your thoughts, feelings and actions are in alignment with your dream, and you obtain the results that you desire when you move from a place of:

- limitation to a place of countless possibilities,

- feeling stuck, dwelling on problems to a place where you find solutions

- 'I can't' mentality to a place of 'how can I.'

As you open up and you change your perception of what is possible for you, you are able to achieve success more easily.

Action step: describe in three words what comes to your mind when you think of your own success

....

....

....

....

....

....

....

....

....

....

....

....

....

Your thoughts, feelings and actions create your results

*"The pessimist sees difficulty in every opportunity.
The optimist sees the opportunity in every difficulty."*

–Winston Churchill

Your thoughts create a certain feeling or emotion and in accordance with the way you feel you will take a particular action and the action you take will dictate your results.

Everything starts from the thought you create in your mind.

For example, if your thought process is: "What if I fail?"

If this is your prevalent thought, you are doomed to fail because this belief will paralyse you and stops you from moving towards the achievement of your goal.

The result will be inaction; you will not take the first step and, as a consequence, you will not achieve what you desire.

To change your results, you must change your paradigm or your attitude, behaviour or multitude of habits. Developing the right success mindset will be instrumental in your own success.

☐

Action step: what results are you getting from your current paradigm?

....

....

....

....

....

....

....

....

....

....

....

....

....

....

....

....

What do you want?

"If you want to conquer fear, don't sit home and think about it. Go out and get busy."

–Dale Carnegie

My mentor Bob Proctor says that the majority of people are extras in their own movie and they allow life to happen to them by sitting on the fence. The reason being is that most people do not know what they want!

What do you want? And what do you want to achieve?

This is your starting point. Your answers will give you a direction and clarity as well as stop you from wanting to move forward aimlessly. I suggest that you return to your end in mind each time you meet confusion and a roadblock along the journey to success.

Once you have identified what you want make the committed decision to stick to it and to do whatever it takes to make it happen.

Action step: what do you want?

....

....

....

....

....

....

....

....

....

....

....

....

....

....

....

....

☐

Action step: what do you want to achieve?

....

....

....

....

....

....

....

....

....

....

....

....

....

....

....

3 ways to catapult your results

"If you don't like something change it. If you can't change it, change your attitude."

–Maya Angelou

If your behaviour is not giving you the results that you desire, change it. There are three ways you can create change:

a) Stop doing what does not work

b) Do more of what works

c) Introduce new things and see if they work

In order to create change, it is very important you do things differently and change your paradigm. You cannot create change using the same habits which created your undesired results in the first place and with the same thinking.

Action step: what could you stop doing?

....

....

....

....

....

....

....

....

....

....

....

....

....

....

....

....

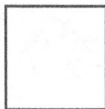

Action step: what could you do more of?

....

....

....

....

....

....

....

Action step: what are the new things you could introduce?

....

....

....

....

....

....

....

How to overcome obstacles on the way

"When you want something badly enough, you will develop the confidence and the ability to overcome any obstacle in your way."

–Brian Tracy

Success is a journey and growth happens through meeting obstacles and failing a few times. Every successful person has failed countless of times; however, it is their persistence that made the difference as well as their willingness to do things differently. It can be very costly to hold onto the old paradigm when a new one is necessary to create better results in your life.

This is particularly true if we look at the way the world is evolving so quickly. In order not to fall behind, we cannot afford to remain stuck in a world which no longer exists. We must keep up with the world as it evolves.

The main point I want to make is that you must learn from your mistakes since this is what will help you move forward and reach a step further in the progressive realisation of your worthy goal.

Whenever you fall down pick yourself up and get back up, again and again and again until you have cracked the code to success.

Action step: what have your learnt from your life experience?

....

....

....

....

....

....

....

....

....

....

....

....

....

....

☐

Action step: what obstacles are getting in the way of your own success?

....

....

....

....

....

....

....

....

....

....

....

....

....

....

....

....

....

DAY 10

Feel the fear and do it anyway

"The fear will never go away as long as I continue to grow."

–Susan Jeffers

When you desire to achieve something, which is bigger than you, you are bound to experience fear. The fear is the fear of the unknown, a false expectation appearing real. When you meet fear, you project something which has not even happened. You create your own story in your head, of not being enough: good enough, experienced enough, beautiful enough, knowledge-able enough, etc.

However, an idea is created twice, first in your mind and then on the physical plane. Therefore, an idea would not come to you if you could not realise it. You are then given a choice to go out there and make it happen. The window of opportunity to realise it is very small; therefore, you must seize it and act on it straight away. If you wait too long, it will be gone and forgotten.

You must acknowledge the fear, push through it, step into the unknown and do what needs to be done anyway. Give yourself permission to explore new possibilities and what seems uncom-fortable.

When you look at your life you must have gone through a lot of things which seem unfamiliar, however, with time, they became familiar and even newly ingrained habits. The path you are on right now is not different.

You will discover that fear is nothing more than a feeling associated with a lack of resources. You fear failing because you do not have all the resources that you need and you do not know how you are going to achieve your dreams. However, the answer is to become resourceful and find the right people who can assist you on your journey. Do not do it alone!

Action step: what lies beyond fear for you?

....

....

....

....

....

....

....

....

....

Be willing to be uncomfortable

"We are all seeking the same thing: everybody wants to fulfil the highest, truest, expression of yourself as a human being. That's what you are looking for."

–Oprah Winfrey

Success lies outside of your comfort zone!

The rewards for growth are outside of your comfort zone. This is where you are most challenged. A challenge is important because it allows you to grow, to stretch and to be the best that you can be.

Remember that humanity's greatest challenge is self-realisation, to live their life to their full potential and to be used fully in order to have no regret at the end of their life.

It's time to
get out of
your comfort zone

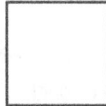

Commit to being willing to be uncomfortable

Exercise: Your Full Commitment Statement

"I am so happy and grateful now that I am willing to do whatever it takes to take my life to the next level and strive."

Signature: ....

Date: ....

Declutter Your Mind

"Nothing binds you except your thoughts. Nothing limits you except your fears. And nothing controls you except your beliefs."

–Marianne Williamson

Since you are creating new habits, the habits of success, it is important that you declutter and free your mind.

In addition to The Essential Guide To Success Checklist, I recommend you write things down in a personal journal and do this powerful exercise I learnt courtesy of Eben Pagan.

Exercise: Freeing The Mind

1. Write down in your personal journal all of your thoughts right now and the things which trouble you or you feel you have to do.

2. Then identify the things that you can control with a star ☆ and the things outside of your control with a circle ●.

3. Prioritise the things that you can control and let go of the things outside of your control for they take too much space in your mind.

By prioritising the things that you can control, you have decluttered your mind of the obsolete and let them go.

Action step: have you decluttered your mind? – Write down the things that you can control (the ones with a star)

....

....

....

....

....

....

....

....

....

....

....

....

....

....

☐

Action step: how do you feel after this exercise?

....

....

....

....

....

....

....

....

....

....

....

....

....

....

....

....

Create the right supportive environment

"Keep only those things that speak to your heart. Then take the plunge and discard all the rest. By doing this, you can reset your life and embark on a new lifestyle."

–Marie Kondo

When you want to achieve success, creating the right environment to support you is important.

Physical nourishment

Being physically fit is crucial for your wellbeing. Your routine for the right physical nourishment should include adequate sleep, exercise, meditation, rest and relaxation and a healthy and balanced diet to nourish your body.

Mental strength

Mental strength is necessary to better cope with overwhelm, obstacles and unforeseen circumstances. Keeping a positive mental attitude (right thoughts + right feelings + right actions = right attitude) will be instrumental.

Supportive external environment

Is your surrounding supportive of your desire for growth? In other words, is your working and living environment clear of clutter and in perfect order?

Clarity starts with order in your mind. Your external environment is a reflection of what is happening inside, so an orderly external environment will reflect an orderly mind.

Moreover, share your goal or dream with people who will support you on your journey. You must avoid sharing your progress with the 'naysayers', people who will discourage you and make you believe that you cannot achieve your goal and that you are 'a big dreamer'.

By sharing your dream with the right like-minded people; people who want to achieve success, you are confirming that you are serious about achieving it and they can hold you accountable for it.

When you change your external environment will change too, it will be a reflection of the many changes you have made internally.

Pascale D. Gibon

☐

Action step: how supportive is your physical nourishment on a scale of 1-10?

....

....

....

....

....

....

....

....

....

....

....

....

....

....

....

☐

Action step: how supportive is your mental strength on a scale of 1-10?

....

....

....

....

....

....

☐

Action step: how supportive is your external environment on a scale of 1-10?

....

....

....

....

....

....

Clear up your messes

"Your ego urges you to accomplish, while the soul merely asks you to enjoy the process."

–Doreen Virtue

Your messes are anything which creates disorder in your life.

A messy desk, a messy office, a messy kitchen, a broken item in need of repair, an item which needs to be thrown away or given away, etc.

There are messes which create clutter which you looked at on Day 13. But, there are also messes which relate to your relationships with others: like an unresolved argument with another person; a past relationship you have not let go of, someone who is seeking your forgiveness or someone you are to apologise to.

☐

Action step: what messes do you need to clear up in your life?

....

....

....

....

....

....

....

....

....

....

....

....

....

....

....

....

Clear up your incompletes

"Your life is your story. Write well. Edit often."

–Lisa Nichols

Clearing up your incompletes is also part of creating the right environment in order to support you on your journey to success.

An incomplete is anything you have started in your life and you have not completed. It could be a course, a project, a book, a relationship, etc.

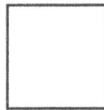

Action step: what are your incompletes?

....

....

....

....

....

....

....

....

....

....

Action step: what do you need to do to clear up your incompletes for closure and by when?

What do you need to do for closure?	By when?

Cultivate a success mindset

"The greatest day in your life and mine is when we take responsibility for our attitudes. That's the day we truly grow up."

–John C. Maxwell

Success starts within and your results will be determined by your attitude (thoughts + feelings + actions.)

- A poor attitude will result in poor results.

- A great attitude will result in great results.

Let me give you an example:

If you have failed at something you might react in two ways:

a) You might have a poor attitude: "Oh no! I have failed, what if I fail again?"

b) You might have a great attitude: "Failure is feedback, I must learn the lessons from this failure and do better next time."

With attitude a) you react; you might make the same mistake again until the lesson is learnt.

With attitude b) you respond; you have grown in awareness and you keep growing.

How long will it take to change and form a new habit?

It will take as long as you want it to take; however, it has been scientifically proven that it takes a minimum of 21 days to form a new habit. On the other hand, through repetition you will be able to cultivate your new awareness and change your results.

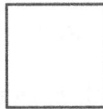

Action step: what is your chosen attitude which is in alignment with the success you want to create?
(remember that your goal is to create a new paradigm)

....

....

....

....

....

....

....

....

....

Create an action mind-set

"Action is a great restorer and builder of confidence. Inaction is not only the result, but the cause, of fear."

–Bob Proctor

There is a small window of execution between the idea you have and the action you take. Have you noticed how ideas can come to you easily; however, if you do not act on them they disappear as quickly as they emerged.

Become action oriented because only an idea which is acted upon and followed through will come to fruition and give you your desired outcome.

If you do not take the right actions, you will not get your desired results. Actions which will quantum leap your results are actions of high value.

☐

Action step: what actions of high value could you take to quantum leap your results?

....

....

....

....

....

....

....

....

....

....

....

....

....

....

....

DAY 18

Map out your clear goals

"Luck is preparation meeting the moment of opportunity."

–Oprah Winfrey

Now that you have identified what you want in order to achieve success, you need to know where you are going. It is important that you become an expert at S.M.A.R.T. goal setting and goal achieving.

- The 5 step method of setting S.M.A.R.T. goals gives you a framework. As you follow this method it reveals that you are serious about fulfilling your desire and that you have a clear vision of your end result. What differentiates people who create change in their life from those who do not is that the former set goals and follow them through to completion.

The S.M.A.R.T model of goal setting is an acronym for:

S = Specific

M = Measurable

A = Attainable

R = Realistic

T = Timely

- Achieving goals means that you have a clear plan to act upon.

It is not enough to set goals you must also work on how you are going to achieve them by taking action.

Research shows that only 13% of us have defined goals; only 3% have their goal in writing and less than 1% review and rewrite their goals on a daily basis.

Action step: what are your S.M.A.R.T goals for this year?

....

....

....

....

....

....

....

....

....

Map your action steps

*"You don't learn to walk by following rules.
You learn by doing, and by falling over."*

–Richard Branson

Now that you have clear S.M.A.R.T goals, you must break them down into specific and clear tasks, activities and actions in order to accomplish your goals.

A clear map of action steps is essential for success. In your map, you identify each step you are to take to reach your destination.

As you work the plan you can assess from your results whether you are on or off course. Therefore, reviewing and adjusting your goals periodically is important.

Action step: what are the necessary action steps you must take to accomplish your goals or dream? (In order to answer this question consider what your next right move should be)

Your S.M.A.R.T goals	Your action steps	Completion date

Identify your resources

"Remember you will not always win. Some days, the most resourceful individual will taste defeat. But there is, in this case, always tomorrow – after you have done your best to achieve success today."

–Maxwell Maltz

I mentioned in Day 10 that to overcome fear you are to become resourceful. Fear of the unknown keeps us stuck and paralysed, but when you become resourceful you act upon your dream or goal and move forward.

Seek the resources that you need in order to become unstuck.

The quality of the questions you ask will determine the quality of your life and results. A great question to ask is:

☐

Action step: what resources do you need to bring your dream or goal to fruition?

What resources do you need?	By when?

DAY 21

Ask for what you want

"If you want something… you have to ask for it!"

–Jack Canfield

One of my mentors, Jack Canfield, says that we do not ask enough for what we want, mainly because we fear being rejected. However, he believes the more we ask the closer we are to accomplishing our dreams.

The Aladdin Factor by Jack Canfield and Mark Victor Hansen is all about asking for what you want. If you do not ask for what you want how can you fulfil your dream or achieve your goals?

Doors will be closed to your asking but doors will also open. Your courage and persistence will be tested in many ways to ensure that you are 100% committed to achieving success.

☐

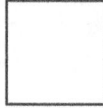

Action step: whom could you ask for help?

Whom could you ask for help?	By when?

Mastermind your way to success

"Coming together is a beginning; keeping together is progress; working together is success."

–Henry Ford

Every successful person is part of a mastermind. It is a misconception to believe that success is achieved alone. Success is always the result of team work effort.

In *Think & Grow Rich*, Napoleon Hill reveals the secrets of success following the study of more than 500 wealthy personalities. Mastermind is one of the secrets. A mastermind group consists of a small group of people between 2 to 5 who get together once a week or twice a month to talk about how they are progressing in relation to their goal achievement plan and what resources they might need to move forward.

Forming a mastermind group is very powerful and results oriented. The purpose of the mastermind is to learn from one another, to share results and to surround yourself with a supportive group of people or one other on your journey to success.

☐

Action step: identify the people you could invite to your mastermind

Whom would you invite to your mastermind group?	By when?

Achieve Your Goals

"A goal is a dream with a deadline."

–Napoleon Hill

There is a difference between goal setting and goal achieving. A number of things must be in place in order to achieve your goals. There is also a belief in the world of personal development that success is 90% mindset and 10% strategy.

So far:

1. You have identified your goals.

2. You have identified your action steps.

3. How do you achieve your goals?

If you are a creative, having a routine or structure in order to improve your productivity might be difficult to follow, but it will be necessary in order to take your life to the next level.

On the other hand, if you are too structured and not flexible enough you might need to be more in the flow.

A balance between structure and being in the flow is what is required.

Without a clear structure not much gets done for you leave room for procrastination. In order for you to be productive and achieve the results that you want you will have to schedule the tasks which provide the greatest value in terms of your desired outcome.

As you focus on the outcomes that you desire you are more likely to achieve your goals.

Action step: what are your desired outcomes in terms of your results?

Desired outcomes	Action steps to be scheduled in your diary

DAY 24

Stay focused

"Successful people maintain a positive focus in life no matter what is going on around them. They stay focused on their past successes rather than their past failures, and on the next action steps they need to take to get them closer to the fulfilment of their goals rather than all the other distractions that life presents to them."

–Jack Canfield

The world we live in is full of distractions, our phone, emails, TV, social media could keep us 'busy' all day! Therefore, it is essential that you remain focused in order to achieve your goal. This is, in my opinion, one of the keys to success.

Spend some time everyday doing the high value tasks which will move you closer to the achievement of your goal.

As you remain focused you put your energy into one thing only at a time. In order to stay focused you will have to create a new routine and new habits.

For example, you could say that you will spend two solid hours writing your book first thing in the morning without checking your phone, emails or social media. Then you could choose a particular time in the day to check your phone, emails or social media.

It is amazing how effective your work can be when you are 100% focused and ignore all distractions. When you are not multi-tasking you are focused.

The end result of this strategy is that you will be very happy at the end of the day because you will have accomplished a lot!

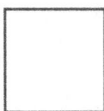

Action step: what do you need to focus on right now to move your dream forward?

....

....

....

....

....

....

....

....

....

....

....

Manage your activities effectively

"The key is not to prioritize what's on your schedule, but to schedule your priorities."

–Stephen Covey

The actions you take will determine the kind of success you achieve. There are activities of a low value and activities of a high value. For example, I mentioned checking social media, even though it is great to interact and connect with others online, it is however a distraction which takes more time than you expect. For example, you look for some information online then you decide to go on one of the social media channels, and before you know it you have spent more time checking messages than you have spent checking what you were looking for! ☺

You can set up a list of about 3 to 6 daily tasks of high value to focus on. You must assign a time to each task to ensure you have a productive day. This activity will help you beat procrastination since you give yourself a command and assign a time to each task.

☐

Action step: how could you better organise your work day?

....

....

....

....

....

....

....

....

....

....

....

....

....

....

....

....

....

Monitor your progress

*"Success leaves clues, and if you sow the same seeds,
you'll reap the same rewards."*

–Brad Thor

How will you know how well you are doing if you do not monitor your progress?

When you monitor your progress you know whether you are on track or not.

Additionally, when you monitor your progress you think about results: are you getting your desired results? If not what adjustments do you need to make?

In order to progress towards your worthy ideal, I have outlined some important questions for you to consider:

- ♥ How are you doing?

- ♥ Is your action plan working and giving you the desired results?

♥ Have you made steady progress or are you at a stand-still?

♥ Do you feel you are on course?

♥ Do you feel inspired and motivated to carry on or do you feel deflated, overwhelmed or stressed out?

☐

Action step: on a scale of 1-10 are you getting your desired results?

....

....

....

....

....

....

....

....

....

....

....

Be disciplined

"Discipline is the bridge between goals and accomplishment."

–Jim Rohn

To be disciplined means that you give yourself a command and you follow it. It is easy to be disciplined when you have a written schedule you can execute daily.

- Successful people wake up early so that they can have a lot done in a day.

    - When are you most alert during the day?

        ☐ in the morning?

        ☐ in the afternoon? or

        ☐ in the evening?

- Successful people never stop learning.

    - Warren Buffet the third richest man in the United States spends three hours a day reading.

- In your daily schedule, you will draw a plan of activities which takes into consideration and consolidates all of the action steps you identified on day 17, 18, 19, 20, 21 and 22.

  - What do you want your days to be filled with?

  - What do you want your daily routine to be?

  - What do you do at a particular time of the day?

Action step: what is your daily schedule on a weekly basis?

(Please draw your most typical weekly schedule)

Time	Mon	Tues	Wed	Thur	Fri	Sat	Sun
05.00-05.30							
05.30-06.00							
06.00-06.30							
06.30-07.00							
07.00-07.30							
07.30-08.00							
08.30-09.00							
09.00-09.30							
09.30-10.00							
10.00-10.30							

Action step: what is your daily schedule on a weekly basis?

Time	Mon	Tues	Wed	Thur	Fri	Sat	Sun
10.30-11.00							
11.00-11.30							
11.30-12.00							
12.00-12.30							
12.30-13.00							
13.00-13.30							
13.30-14.00							
14.00-14.30							
14.30-15.00							
15.00-15.30							
15.30-16.00							
16.00-16.30							
16.30-17.00							
17.00-17.30							
17.30-18.00							
18.00-18.30							
18.30-19.00							
19.00-19.30							
19.30-20.00							
20.00-20.30							
20.30-21.00							

Rinse and repeat the cycle of excellence

"Excellence is an art won by training and habituation. We do not act rightly because we have virtue or excellence, but we rather have those because we have acted rightly. We are what we repeatedly do. Excellence then, is not an act but a habit."

–Aristotle

Excellence is the ability to bring something to completion. As you go through the 30-Day Challenge to Building Your Path to Success and Fulfilling Your Life's Purpose, once you have achieved your dream, you can apply the same cycle of excellence (courtesy of Jack Canfield) to your next goal or dream.

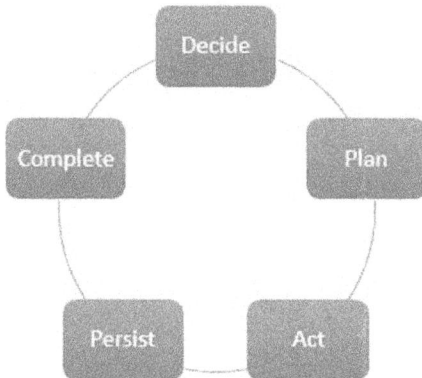

☐

Action step: complete the cycle or excellence

1. Decide what you want

2. Plan your action steps

3. Act on your action steps

4. Persist with your end in mind

5. Complete your plan of action

DAY 29

Be grateful

"It's a funny thing about life, once you begin to take note of the things you are grateful for, you begin to lose sight of the things that you lack."

–Germany Kent

Be grateful for where you are right now, for your new awareness and for what is to come. You have chosen to let go of the past in order to create something new and secure a better future. This is commendable.

However, it is from a place of gratefulness that you strengthen your faith and belief and you expand to new possibilities.

Be grateful for the opportunity for growth.

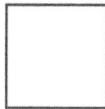

Exercise: Gratefulness

- Take some time each day to pause and reflect on what you are grateful for in your life no matter how big or small.

- Make a list in your personal journal or say out loud daily 10 things you are grateful for.

☐ **What are your grateful for?**

	What are you grateful for every day?
1.	
2.	
3.	
4.	
5.	
6.	
7.	
8.	
9.	
10.	

Celebrate your successes

*"The more you praise and celebrate your life,
the more there is in life to celebrate."*

–Oprah Winfrey

Congratulations! You have reached the end of the Essential Guide To Success Checklist and lived up to the 30-Day Challenge to Build your Path to Success and Fulfil Your Life's Purpose.

You have come a long way from the day you decided to transform your life and experience success to now.

As you move confidently in the direction of your dreams, uplift your spirit by celebrating each win on your way to achieving your goals for real success is the journey you go through.

The joy is in the journey: when you reach the top of the mountain you usually start thinking of your next challenge. Therefore, when you succeed and reach the mountain top enjoy this moment as an extraordinary one, you did it! You could have thrown in the towel; you could have said 'no' but instead you made it happen! This is worth celebrating.

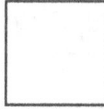

Action step: what success do you wish to celebrate today?

Your Successes List	
🦋	
🦋	
🦋	
🦋	
🦋	
🦋	
🦋	
🦋	
🦋	
🦋	

SUMMARY OF THE SUCCESS CHECKLIST ACTIVITIES

- ☐ **Day 1**   What does success mean to you?

- ☐ **Day 2**   What are you passionate about?

- ☐ **Day 3**   Who are the successful people you could model?

- ☐ **Day 4**   Take 100% responsibility for your results

- ☐ **Day 5**   You become what you think about

- ☐ **Day 6**   Your thoughts, feelings and actions create your results

- ☐ **Day 7**   What do you want?

- ☐ **Day 8**   What could you stop doing?

  What could you do more of?

  What are the new things you could introduce?

- ☐ **Day 9**   What have you learnt from your life experience?

  What obstacles are getting in the way of your own success?

- ☐ **Day 10** What lies beyond fear for you?

☐ **Day 11**   Be willing to be uncomfortable

☐ **Day 12**   Declutter your mind

☐ **Day 13**   Create the right supportive environment

☐ **Day 14**   What messes do you need to clear up in your life?

☐ **Day 15**   What are your incompletes

What do you need to do to clear up your incompletes and by when?

☐ **Day 16**   Cultivate a success mindset

☐ **Day 17**   What actions of high value could you take to quantum leap your results?

☐ **Day 18**   What are your S.M.A.R.T goals for this year?

☐ **Day 19**   Map out your action steps

☐ **Day 20**   What resources do you need?

☐ **Day 21**   Ask for what you want

☐ **Day 22**   Whom would you invite to your Mastermind group?

☐ **Day 23**   Achieve your goals

☐ **Day 24**   What do you need to focus on right now to move your dream forward?

☐ **Day 25**   Manage your activities effectively

☐ **Day 26**   Monitor your progress

☐ **Day 27**   What is your daily schedule on a weekly basis?

☐ **Day 28**   Rinse and repeat the cycle of excellence

☐ **Day 29**   What are you grateful for every day?

☐ **Day 30**   Celebrate your successes

Pascale D. Gibon

NOTES

....

....

....

....

....

....

....

....

....

....

....

....

....

....

....

....

....

....

....

....

....

....

NOTES

....
....
....
....
....
....
....
....
....
....
....
....
....
....
....
....
....
....
....
....
....
....

SPECIAL INVITATION FROM PASCALE

I am here to serve you as your Change Catalyst, Transformational and Success Life Coach.

I know that the road to success may feel like a lonely experience, I have been there myself. You might feel unsupported during your transformation process. I want you to know that nothing is achieved without the support of others. Therefore, I invite you to join our wonderful community of like-minded people who have chosen to live beyond fear and say Yes! to love, happiness and success.

I invite you to join our 'Path to Success Checklist' private Facebook group where you will receive all the support that you need from our community. You can share your own experience, breakthroughs, ask questions and receive valuable information.

I moderate and check our Facebook community on a regular basis.

I invite you also to contact me directly by email: pascale@pascalegibon.com, leave a comment or ask a question. I will be very happy to help you and to connect with you.

Join our private community on Facebook:
http://bit.ly/Pathtosuccesschecklist

Connect with me on Twitter:
https://www.twitter.com/pascalegibon

Connect with me on LinkedIn: http://bit.ly/pascalelinkedin

Follow me on Instagram:
https:// www.instagram.com/pascalegibon

Follow me on YouTube: https://www.youtube.com/pascalegibon

Listen to my podcast: The Everyday Life Balance Show
http://bit.ly/ELBSPodcast

on iTunes: http://bit.ly/id1247430885

on Stitcher radio: http://bit.ly/ELBStitcher

To your success and happiness!

With love and gratitude

Pascale Gibon

Your Change Catalyst

ABOUT PASCALE GIBON

- Pascale Gibon is the #1 best-selling Author of YES! TO Love™ - The Ultimate Guide to Personal Transformation for Everyday Life Balance.

- She is a Certified Jack Canfield Trainer in the Success Principles, a Licensed LifeSuccess Consultant, A Master Results Coach, and a Passion Test Facilitator. She has been teaching personal development as an International Transformational and Success Trainer since 2009.

- Pascale Gibon is also the Founder of YES! TO Training (Y.T.T - YES! to True Transformation), your self-empowerment portal for transformation which has been designed to help you be the best that you can be and achieve your dreams with courage and confidence.

- YES! TO Love Academy is the umbrella for her live events where she takes you through deep transformation through her various workshops.

- Known as a 'Change Catalyst', Pascale Gibon is highly intuitive and she has the particular talent of helping you walk 100% in your greatness with confidence and harness your unique divine gifts and talents so that you can live your life to your fullest potential, be the best that you can be and live a life of love.

  As a visionary and creative, her life purpose is to inspire and empower you and guide you to happiness through love and joy in the context of understanding and compassion.

  Pascale Gibon can be contacted at pascale@pascalegibon.com.

OTHER RESOURCES

Other books by Pascale
YES! TO Love – The Ultimate Guide to Personal Transformation for Everyday Life Balance

YES! TO Training Online Courses
- The Courage to Rise and Shine Programme
- The 30 Day Success Checklist Audio Course

Personalised Private Coaching
- To book a discovery call with Pascale
  https://www.pascalegibon.com/p/private-coaching

YES! TO LOVE Academy Live Training
- Saying YES! TO Love
- Walking the Golden Path to Success
- Breakthrough to Greatness

Free resources
- The Top 10 Success Habits to Create Lasting and Positive Change Workbook.
- The 7 Key Principles To Achieve Your Dreams 3-Part Video Series.

Blog articles with useful tips and strategies
http://bit.ly/PascaleBlog

The Everyday Life Balance Show
The podcast for men and women who want to create more balance in their life on a mental, physical and spiritual level.
Listen on iTunes: http://bit.ly/id1247430885
Listen on Stitcher Radio: http://bit.ly/ELBStitcher

ACKNOWLEDGMENTS

I would like to express my heartfelt gratitude and abiding thanks to the following people for their love, support and teachings:

The Almighty God

My family and friends for their everlasting support and unconditional love.

Master Ruyho Okawa for teaching me the laws of happiness.

My amazing mentors who have taught me about success and how to become the best that I can be: Bob Proctor, Doreen Virtue, Raymond Aaron, Jack Canfield, Lisa Nichols, Janet-Bray Attwood, Marci Shimoff, Debra Poneman, Wayne Dyer, Chris Gardner, Brendon Burchard, Mike Dillard, Eben Pagan, Antony Robbins, Oprah Winfrey, Les Brown, Napoleon Hill, Marianne Williamson, Marcia Wieder, Marie Manin Morissey, Earl Nightingale, Robert Kiyosaki and Sharon Lechter.

My students for their willingness to learn, grow and step outside of their comfort zone.

My readers, listeners, clients and customers for making it possible for me to live a purposeful life, grow and experience joy, every single day.

www.ingramcontent.com/pod-product-compliance
Lightning Source LLC
Chambersburg PA
CBHW062018040426
42447CB00010B/2056